# The Wilderness Road

## by Sarah De Capua

Content Adviser: Dr. Michael A. Lofaro,
Professor of American Literature and American Studies,
University of Tennessee

Reading Adviser: Susan Kesselring, M.A.,
Literacy Educator,
Rosemount–Apple Valley–Eagan (Minnesota) School District

**COMPASS POINT BOOKS**
**MINNEAPOLIS, MINNESOTA**

Compass Point Books
3109 West 50th Street, #115
Minneapolis, MN 55410

Visit Compass Point Books on the Internet at *www.compasspointbooks.com*
or e-mail your request to *custserv@compasspointbooks.com*

On the cover: William Tylee Ranney's painting *Boone's First View of Kentucky*, shows Daniel Boone (center) after crossing the Appalachian Mountains with a group of explorers.

Photographs ©: Courtesy of The Anschutz Collection, photo by William J. O'Connor, cover; Prints Old and Rare, back cover (far left); Library of Congress, back cover; David Muench/Corbis, 5, 40; North Wind Picture Archives, 6, 9, 19, 33, 38; Hulton Archive/Getty Images, 8; MPI/Getty Images, 11, 12, 29; Canadian Heritage Gallery #23005/National Archives of Canada C-140172, 13; The Granger Collection, New York, 15, 21, 27, 30, 35; Art by Mike Smith, courtesy of SmithDRay Web Pages, 16; Nancy Carter/North Wind Picture Archives, 17; Courtesy of Picture History, 22; The Stapleton Collection/The Bridgeman Art Library, 37.

Editor: Nick Healy
Page Production: The Design Lab
Photo Researchers: Bobbie Nuytten and Svetlana Zhurkin
Cartographer: XNR Productions, Inc.
Library Consultant: Kathleen Baxter

Creative Director: Keith Griffin
Editorial Director: Carol Jones
Managing Editor: Catherine Neitge

*For Christopher, a modern-day Daniel Boone. SED*

**Library of Congress Cataloging-in-Publication Data**
De Capua, Sarah
 The Wilderness Road / by Sarah De Capua.
   p. cm.—(We the people)
 Includes bibliographical references and index.
 ISBN 0-7565-1637-4 (hard cover)
 1. Boone, Daniel, 1734-1820—Juvenile literature. 2. Frontier and pioneer life—Kentucky—Juvenile literature. 3. Frontier and pioneer life—Tennessee, East—Juvenile literature. 4. Frontier and pioneer life—Virginia—Juvenile literature. 5. Wilderness Road—Juvenile literature. 6. Kentucky—Description and travel—Juvenile literature. 7. Tennessee, East—Description and travel—Juvenile literature. 8. Virginia—Description and travel—Juvenile literature. I. Title. II. We the people (Series) (Compass Point Books)
 F454.D4 2006
 973.2—dc22                    2005027563

# TABLE OF CONTENTS

# THE PROMISE OF THE WEST

In 1700, the Declaration of Independence and the American Revolution were still many years away. The Louisiana Purchase of 1803 and the Lewis and Clark expedition that followed were historic milestones that would not occur for another century. But British colonists had been living along the eastern coast of North America for nearly 100 years.

As more Europeans—mostly British, Germans, and Irish—crossed the Atlantic to settle on small farms in the colonies, the East Coast became increasingly crowded. People longed for more land, where they could live and grow crops to feed their families and to make a living. They turned their hopes west, toward the vast wilderness of the North American continent.

At that time, the settled areas included land between the Atlantic coast and the Appalachian Mountains. The Appalachians lie between 100 and 300 miles (160 and

4

*The dense woods of the Appalachian Mountains made exploration challenging.*

480 kilometers) west of the coast. They extend about 1,500 miles (2,400 km), from Alabama in the south to the Canadian province of Quebec in the north. For colonial Americans, the Appalachians formed a natural barrier separating the East and the Mississippi River valley. The land between the mountains and the Mississippi River was the first American West, a difficult but fertile frontier that would eventually attract settlers in great numbers.

Explorers, hunters, and traders reported thick forests and good farmland beyond the mountains. One explorer, General Abraham Wood, was the commander of Fort Henry, near present-day Petersburg, Virginia.

*A party of pioneers enters the wilderness on horseback.*

Around 1700, Wood explored the region with five other men and an American Indian guide. A member of his party kept a diary in which he described "exceeding rich Land that [yields] two Crops of Indian Corne a yeare and … timber trees … [in] abundance."

By the mid-1700s, tales of what lay beyond the mountains were spreading among colonists, mostly by word of mouth, newspapers, and handbills. Colonists knew there was plenty of wildlife in the forests and grasslands. Buffalo, deer, turkeys, bears, elk, and birds would provide plenty of food. Forests of ash, oak, walnut, pine, and cherry meant a vast supply of wood to build cabins, barns, and corrals for farm animals. Trout, perch, and bass filled streams, lakes, and rivers. Mink, otters, beavers, raccoons, and foxes would supply many furs for trade.

The Cherokee Indian name for the land beyond the Appalachians was *Kentahthe*. This word may have meant "meadowland," "land of tomorrow," or "the land where we will live." Colonists began to call it Caintuck, Kaintucke, or Kentucky. The name applied to a large area beyond the mountains, much larger than the present-day state of Kentucky.

There were few permanent settlers there in the mid-1700s, which made it sound like an ideal place to colonists who desired more land. The area also appealed to land speculators, who hoped to make huge fortunes by acquiring large tracts of land and then selling it at a profit to settlers.

*Daniel Boone*

While routes through the Appalachians already existed, especially in what would become the northeastern United States, these were mostly buffalo traces, or trails, that had also been used for hundreds of years by Indians. Southern routes through the mountains became necessary as Eastern colonies grew in population. In 1775, a group of men led by Daniel Boone cleared a new route to Kentucky. Parts of the path were Indian footpaths and trails worn by animals. Boone and his men widened and straightened those sections, and cleared new stretches through the woods. The group made what would later be called the Wilderness Road. It became one of the most heavily traveled routes, and it eased the westward expansion of the United States—into Kentucky and beyond.

# PARADISE BEYOND THE APPALACHIANS

Throughout the 1700s, accounts of Kentucky as a paradise spread and increased in number. Many stories sounded too good to be true and were, in fact, tall tales. For example, some people said there was no winter there and crops grew year-round. Still, many Easterners were eager to move to Kentucky.

Settlement of Kentucky would not be easy, however. Natural and political barriers stood in the way. Merely getting there was a major challenge. There was no easily traveled road through the mountains. There were winding trails, but they were hard to follow and too narrow.

*Hunters returned from Kentucky with tales of plentiful game.*

They could not serve as a route for wagons and the pack animals that would carry settlers' belongings. But even if colonists could make the difficult trip, western land was not free for the taking. The French and British governments claimed rights to the area, sometimes laying claim to the same pieces of land. In addition, American Indians intended to protect their traditional hunting lands from being taken over by colonists.

Back in the late 1600s, French explorers first claimed the region between the Appalachians and the Mississippi River. The French wanted to keep English colonists and European immigrants off their land. French government officials in Louisiana went so far as to imprison British exploration parties in New Orleans. They held explorers—sometimes for as long as two years—to discourage settlement.

The British eventually battled the French for control of North America. Both sides sought the help of Indian tribes, and the conflict became known as the French and

*A group of American Indians under French command ambush British troops during the French and Indian War.*

Indian War (1754–1763). The British made agreements with the Cherokee, Shawnee, Delaware, and other tribes to fight against the French. In exchange for Indian help, the British agreed that if they won the war, they would settle only small areas of land west of the Appalachians.

When the war ended, the victorious British gained control of all North American lands east of the

*In their defeat, the French lost a large area of North American territory.*

Mississippi River. However, colonists found it was no easier for them to settle Kentucky and other areas between the Appalachians and the Mississippi. One reason was that their own government, the British Parliament, did not want them there. Parliament issued the Proclamation of 1763, which forbade colonists from moving west of the Appalachians. Parliament declared the area a reserve for Indians. The order would be nearly impossible for the British to enforce, and colonists largely ignored it. Still, large numbers of Americans did not settle west of the

Appalachians until after their defeat of the British in the Revolutionary War (1775–1783). At that time, the main obstacle holding colonists back was the difficulty of travel.

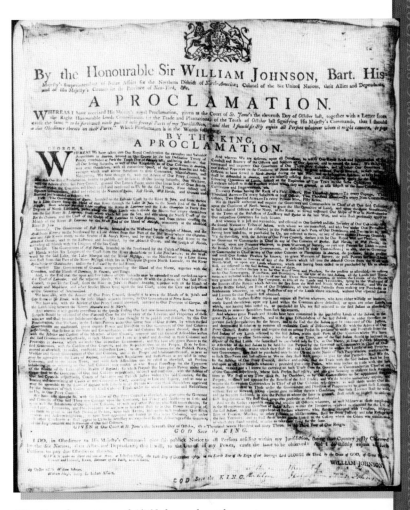

*The Proclamation of 1763 barred settlement west of the Appalachian Mountains.*

An important step toward finding a good route through the mountains had been taken in 1750. That year, Dr. Thomas Walker set out to make the vast possibilities of Kentucky settlement a reality. He and a group of men crossed the Appalachians, beginning their journey

13

near present-day Kingsport, Tennessee. Walker wanted to explore 800,000 acres (320,000 hectares) of land owned by the Loyal Land Company of Virginia. The company was owned by a group of London businessmen.

Walker became the first white man to describe a place he named Cave Gap. It was almost like a natural path to the other side of the mountains. Walker described the gap in his diary: "We went four miles to a large creek … and from [there] six miles to Cave Gap, the land being level." The relatively flat land made travel much easier for the explorers.

Walker also noted "a plain Indian road" through the area. The Indian road was part of the Warrior's Path, which was originally a buffalo trace. Large roaming herds of buffalo had worn the path through the thick woods. Indians called it *Athawominee* and used it to travel to hunting and battle grounds. The path ran from present-day New York to South Carolina, connecting with paths going in many directions.

*Cumberland Gap provided a natural path through the mountains.*

It would take years before Walker's discoveries would aid settlement beyond the Appalachians. Cave Gap, later known as Cumberland Gap, would become the main route through the mountains. And long stretches of the Warrior's Path would become part of the Wilderness Road, which would carry thousands of settlers into Kentucky.

15

# DREAMS OF TRANSYLVANIA

In the spring of 1775, a retired North Carolina judge named Richard Henderson met with Cherokee leaders. The meeting was held at Sycamore Shoals on the Watauga River, near the spot where the present-day borders of Tennessee, North Carolina, and Virginia meet. Henderson convinced Cherokee leaders to sell him about 20 million acres (8 million hectares) of property. One chief named Dragging Canoe stood against the treaty and warned of the trouble that settlement of Kentucky would bring. The other Cherokee leaders ignored Dragging Canoe. The exchange became known as the Treaty of Sycamore Shoals.

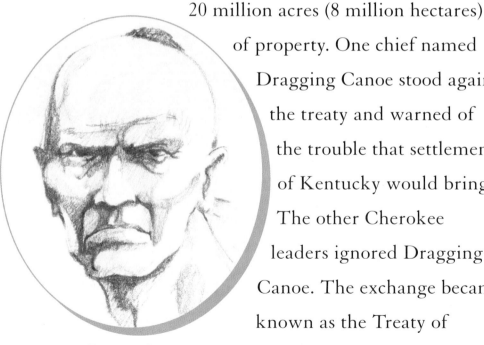

*Dragging Canoe*

Henderson's arrangement was not without problems. Legally, the Cherokee did not own the land. They did not hold a deed that would be honored by either the British or colonial governments. However, those facts did not stop Henderson from making the deal with the Cherokee.

*Settlement of Kentucky would require clearing of roads through the woods.*

The Cherokee gave Henderson most of Kentucky and other land beyond the Appalachian Mountains. In exchange, they received clothing, tools, flour, guns, and trade goods, plus a cash payment. The Cherokee also gave him the right to make a road through tribal grounds to his land.

Henderson was thrilled with his purchase. His dream was to establish a 14th American colony called

**17**

Transylvania. The previous winter, Henderson had issued ads that offered free land to settlers of his colony. Every settler who promised to raise a crop of corn and to protect against Indian attacks would receive 500 acres (200 hectares). Henderson also promised land to people who established ironworks, salt factories, and sawmills. And he offered to reward the settler who raised the largest crop of corn and the settler who brought the largest herd of sheep. Each would receive as much as 500 additional acres (200 hectares) of property. Fifty soldiers would be hired for the "protection of the Settlers of the Country" and would receive 500 acres (200 hectares) and a small amount of cash as payment.

Stories of the natural wonders of Kentucky, along with offers of free land, convinced many settlers to pack up and move. But Henderson still had to do something to help people get through the mountains. He decided to hire a man named Daniel Boone to clear a road for settlers. With that move, Henderson's dream of Transylvania and colonists' dreams of settling in paradise seemed one step closer to reality.

Born in Pennsylvania in 1734, Daniel Boone was a skilled frontiersman. He had learned about hunting and survival in the wilderness by watching his family members and practicing on his own. He had always lived close to the frontier, first in Pennsylvania and later in North Carolina. During the French and Indian War, Boone worked as a wagon driver, and he met a soldier named John Findlay, who told him about Kentucky. Boone longed to see it for himself.

*John Findlay was an early explorer of the region west of the Appalachian Mountains.*

**19**

After the war, Boone's life changed in two important ways. He married Rebecca Bryan, with whom he eventually had 10 children, and he took his first hunting trip to Kentucky.

That trip took place in 1769. When Boone returned two years later, he was determined to move his family there. But that would not happen until 1775. First, he would have to clear the Wilderness Road, a task that Henderson had assigned to him.

Henderson's dream of a new colony called Transylvania would never come true. However, his decision to hire Boone had a lasting impact. Boone's work would open Kentucky to settlement and gain him a place among those most responsible for western movement in the United States.

# BUILDING THE WILDERNESS ROAD

Daniel Boone had a difficult job to do. He and his party of 30 axmen—including his brother, Squire—were to cut a road through the Cumberland Gap to Kentucky. Boone required that all the men with him be physically strong and knowledgeable about survival in the wilderness. On March 10, 1775, the men started west from the place where the Great Philadelphia Wagon Road met the Holston River, in present-day southwestern Virginia. (The Great

*Daniel Boone led settlers west through the mountains and into Kentucky.*

21

*Daniel Boone's party advances through the woods as men at the front clear the way.*

Philadelphia Wagon Road ran from Philadelphia south to Big Lick, Virginia, now called Roanoke.)

From the beginning, the journey was difficult. The men mostly followed buffalo traces and Indian paths, straightening the route and clearing brush along the way.

Throughout the 200-mile (320-km) journey, streams, mountains, and thickets of bushes and cane stood in their way. The men also worried about conflicts with Indians, particularly the Shawnee.

Boone and his group made steady progress. They went through Moccasin Gap near the present-day border between Virginia and Kentucky. Continuing west, they traveled beyond the Clinch River, Powell Mountain, and the Powell River. Boone rode slightly ahead of the others. He marked the trees to show the route the axmen should follow. Progress was slow as axmen cut away brush, vines, and small trees. Other men dragged fallen trees out of the way, cut through cane, and burned dead brush. The men had to work through swift-flowing streams. (They named one stream Troublesome Creek because they had such a hard time crossing it.) Rain, snow, deep mud, and steep mountain climbs made their job more difficult. At night, they rested around a campfire and cooked wild game they had hunted during the day.

In a valley where the Cumberland Mountains (a section of the Appalachians) lay before them, Boone's crew cut new road for about 20 miles (32 km). They stopped at Martin's Station, a small settlement founded by Joseph Martin, where they got fresh supplies and took a short rest. When they resumed their work, the men continued through the valley for 25 miles (40 km) to Cumberland Gap. They cut through to the Warrior's Path described years earlier by Dr. Thomas Walker. Boone's group then followed the path to the Cumberland River. This part of the journey went quickly, since the path was already well-worn and cleared of most trees and brush.

After crossing the Cumberland River, the journey became more difficult again. Working through low-growing trees and thick brush, they progressed—sometimes only a few feet at a time—to the Laurel River. They went beyond the Laurel River and then the Rockcastle River. For 30 more miles (48 km), the men chopped their way until they reached the far side of the Cumberland Gap.

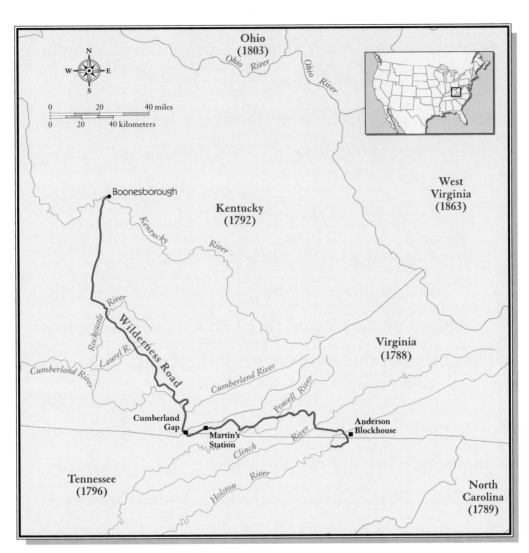

*Boone and his men carved a route through mountain passes and across rivers.*

On March 22, the men came out of the mountains and shouted for joy. They looked upon the plains of Kentucky stretched out for miles ahead of them. Felix

Walker, one of Boone's axmen, kept a journal throughout the adventure. In it, he described his feelings and those of his fellow axmen, on seeing Kentucky for the first time. "Every heart abounded with joy & excitement," he wrote. "[The] new Country was a dazzling object with many of our Company. ... So Rich a Soil we had never [seen] before, Covered with Clover in full Bloom."

Though Boone and his party had been physically challenged by the terrain, they had not seen any Indians. They believed this was because of the Treaty of Sycamore Shoals. Exhausted from their work, members of Boone's party made a camp just outside present-day Richmond, Kentucky. They did not post a guard. Two nights later, on March 24, the Shawnee attacked. They killed two of Boone's men, wounded two others, and stole some horses. Three days later, the Shawnee attacked again, this time killing two and wounding three. Afterward, Boone and the remaining men moved to a spot near the Kentucky River. By April 6, they had constructed a new settlement

*A drawing of Boonesborough, the first settlement in Kentucky*

surrounded by a protective fort. They named the settlement Boonesborough.

The road carved by Boone and his men was first known as Boone's Trace. The route gained its more famous name—the Wilderness Road—once settlers began traveling it by the thousands.

# MOVING TO KENTUCKY

When the Treaty of Sycamore Shoals was signed years earlier, the Cherokee chief named Dragging Canoe had said, "You have bought a fair land, but there is a cloud hanging over it. You will find its settlement dark and bloody." The early settlers who traveled the Wilderness Road found Dragging Canoe's warning had been correct.

The Shawnee and Cherokee people fought to drive out the settlers. War parties raided settlements, killing families, stealing farm animals, and burning down barns and cabins. Raids on Boonesborough continued regularly. During the American Revolution, several Indian tribes supported the British. In return, the British supplied the tribes with weapons. This only made attacks on Kentucky settlers more dangerous and bloody. For some in Boonesborough and other small settlements, the raids were too much to endure. Many settlers took the Wilderness Road back East.

*Kentucky settlers fight off an attack on Boonesborough.*

Even after the Revolutionary War, western settlement
was dangerous. Still, thousands of Americans refused to give
up their dream of a new life on the frontier. Moving west
required much preparation. Settlers packed food, clothing,
blankets, tools, and cooking equipment into their covered
wagons. They sometimes traded for or bought oxen to pull

*A group of settlers heads into the frontier with their heavily loaded wagons and livestock.*

the wagons. Oxen were stronger than horses for the long, difficult journey through the mountains.

Settlers who were headed for Kentucky gathered at the Anderson Blockhouse, in southern Virginia. Most settlers preferred traveling in large groups because they believed they would be protected from Indian attacks. From the blockhouse, the settlers traveled by wagon to the Cumberland Gap. Until the road was widened to 30 feet (9.2 meters) in 1795, wagons had to be left at Martin's Station, on the east side of the gap. The settlers loaded their belongings onto pack animals and rode or walked from there. Sometimes, the single-file line of settlers stretched for 2 miles (3.2 km) along the trail. Every mile of the journey held its own difficulties. Settlers had to go up mountainsides, walk across swift-flowing streams, and trudge through swamps. When Richard Henderson first made the trip, he wrote, "No part of the road [was] tolerable. ... Most of it [was] either hilly, stony, [or] slippery."

Each day on the road brought new challenges as well. Pack animals lost their loads in rivers. Children got lost in the woods. Cattle and sheep wandered off, drowned in swollen rivers, or were attacked at night by wolves or coyotes. Rain kept the settlers from making fires for cooking and warmth. Measles and dysentery sometimes sickened them. Tragedy threatened one party that made the journey in 1784, when a swift river current nearly swept away a young mother carrying her two children in her arms. And always, there were the frightening stories about settlers on the trail ahead of them who had been killed by Indians.

Once in Kentucky, the travelers came to a fork in the Wilderness Road. To the north lay Boonesborough, Winchester, and Lexington. To the west were Crab Orchard, Logan's Station (present-day Stanford), and Harrodsburg. Later, the road was extended until it ended at the Ohio River, at today's Louisville, Kentucky. Settlers could then float down the Ohio on flatboats.

The Wilderness Road was the most popular route west for settlers from Virginia, North Carolina, and South Carolina, as well as those from as far north as Maryland, New Jersey, and Pennsylvania. Despite the difficulty, more than 70,000 people traveled the road between 1775 and 1795.

# FROM WILDERNESS TO STATEHOOD

"When we first arrived there were few inhabitants," wrote Dan Drake, whose family settled in Kentucky in 1788, when he was 10 years old. "Within six years the number of settlers had increased so that one could not wander a mile in any direction without coming upon another cabin." Drake, who recorded these thoughts in his diary, went on to become a famous doctor and teacher.

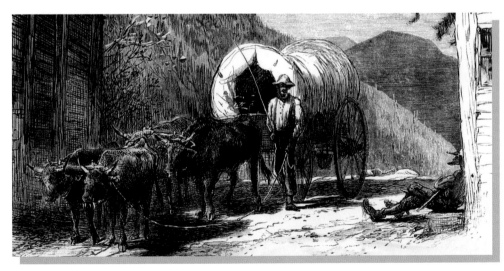

*A covered wagon follows the Wilderness Road.*

Settlers like Drake's family may have poured into Kentucky believing it was paradise. They soon learned they would face hardship and difficulty just to survive. Settlers moved onto plots of land that were anywhere from 38 to 10,000 acres (15.2 to 4,000 hectares). On a very large plot, however, usually no more than 40 acres (16 hectares) could be cleared at a time, if the settler hoped to keep the plowing and gardening manageable and to keep the soil fresh.

Horses, cattle, goats, and other grazing animals were moved from pasture to pasture. Settlers raised hogs and chickens as well. They grew melons, turnips, corn, beans, squash, and pumpkins. As farms grew in size, farmers planted hemp, tobacco, and wheat as cash crops. These crops—as well as livestock, furs, and animal skins—would be sold and shipped back East over the Wilderness Road.

Family cabins were usually one-room structures that measured no more than 16 feet by 20 feet (4.9 m by 6.1 m). They were made by stacking logs of hickory, oak, pine, or walnut. Red clay and moss were jammed between the logs

*Kentucky settlers built log cabins, grew crops, and hunted for food.*

to keep out insects and cold air. A door and windows were
cut in after all the logs were in place. Tables, chairs, beds,
and washstands were made from the same wood as the
cabin. A fireplace of large, flat stones held together with
mud plaster completed the home.

At first, Kentucky was made up of scattered clusters of a few cabins. After a while, more families arrived and built cabins, turning the clusters into settlements. A typical settlement consisted of a store, tavern, schoolhouse, church, and five to 10 cabins. Away from a settlement, families built small forts called stations. Each station was protected by a large wooden gate that could be closed during Indian attacks. Men stuck the barrels of their rifles through narrow openings in the fort's walls to fire on raiders.

In 1792, Kentucky became the 15th state. By then, the population of Kentucky, which had been only a few hundred in 1780, was 75,000. In 1800, the population reached 221,000.

Isaac Shelby was the first governor of Kentucky. In 1795, he ordered the Wilderness Road to be widened to 30 feet (9.2 m) across. This would allow the wagons to travel the entire length of the road. When the work was finished in October 1796, Kentucky's businesses and people were able to move goods easily to and from the Eastern states.

*Isaac Shelby*

Between 1795 and 1810, as many as 300,000 settlers made the journey to the frontier. Although it was wider, the Wilderness Road still presented many problems for travelers. It was filled with bumps and holes. Wooden wagon wheels often broke or got stuck in deep holes. Horses and oxen—valuable pack animals—could stumble and break a leg, which could be devastating for a farm family. Many places along the road were still very steep and muddy.

Settlers began to take other routes west. By the early 1800s, work had been finished on the Pennsylvania Road, which connected Philadelphia to Pittsburgh. It was one of the first gravel roads in the country. Some settlers traveling west took this road to Pittsburgh, then floated on flatboats or rafts down the Ohio River to Kentucky.

Other travelers used the National Road, which was also known as the National Pike or the Cumberland Road. Made of crushed stone, it was the nation's first federal highway. The first portion of the road was completed in 1818. It connected the Potomac River in Maryland with the Ohio River. At the Ohio River, settlers loaded their belongings onto flatboats and floated down the river to Kentucky.

*Settlers travel down the Ohio River by flatboat.*

# TODAY'S WILDERNESS ROAD

Much of the Wilderness Road no longer exists. Homes, buildings, and farms, as well as modern roads and highways, have been built on top of the original route. Portions of the road still exist, though, and can be found in parks and forests. People walk, bike, and ride horses along the road. Some are not even aware that they are on such a famous trail.

In 1940, the Cumberland Gap National Historical Park was created to preserve part of the Wilderness Road. This 21,000-acre (8,400-hectare) park is located where the Virginia, Kentucky, and Tennessee state lines meet. It includes a portion of the Wilderness Road and Cumberland Gap.

In 1996, the National Park Service, which is responsible for Cumberland Gap National Historical Park, built two tunnels through the Cumberland Mountains. Each tunnel is 4,600 feet (1,403 m) long. The tunnels cut through the mountains near Cumberland Gap and provide car travel that is safer than the previous route, which was a narrow highway with many sharp curves.

In the early 2000s, National Park Service officials also worked to restore the Wilderness Road through

*Thousands of Americans traveled the Wilderness Road to Kentucky, a land full of promise.*

Cumberland Gap so it would look the way it did between 1780 and 1810. This stretch of road, which had previously been paved, was torn up and replaced with several tons of dirt. More than 20,000 trees were planted in the area to re-create the dense forest that settlers traveled through on the way west.

In southwestern Virginia, Wilderness Road State Park is the home of Martin's Station, a living-history museum. Workers dressed as pioneers show visitors what life was like on the Virginia frontier in 1775. The park also includes a trail that follows the route of Boone and his axmen from Martin's Station to Cumberland Gap. In mid-2005, a monument was erected near Martin's Station. It honors Joseph Martin and the pioneers who traveled along the Wilderness Road to start new lives in the Western lands of the young United States.

# GLOSSARY

**axmen**—workers who are skilled at using an ax

**blockhouse**—a small building designed to be easily protected from attack

**dysentery**—an infection that causes severe diarrhea

**federal**—having to do with the nation

**flatboats**—boats with a flat bottom and square ends, used for transporting freight in shallow water

**frontiersman**—a person who is skilled at living outside settled land

**handbills**—single pieces of paper with messages on them, like fliers

**ironworks**—a building where iron or steel products are made

**speculators**—people who buy goods or property with the expectation of selling at a higher price in the future

# DID YOU KNOW?

- One of the founders of the Loyal Land Company of Virginia was Peter Jefferson, the father of future U.S. president Thomas Jefferson.

- The governors of Virginia and North Carolina declared Richard Henderson's purchase of Kentucky illegal. By the end of the Revolution, his dream of Transylvania was over.

- A settlement, such as Boonesborough, was considered permanent only if women and children lived there.

- By 1820, 1 million of the nation's 10 million people lived in Kentucky and Tennessee.

# IMPORTANT DATES

## Timeline

| | |
|---|---|
| **1750** | Dr. Thomas Walker and his crew find the Warrior's Path, cross into Kentucky, and name Cave Gap and the Cumberland River. |
| **1775** | Cherokee leaders sign the Treaty of Sycamore Shoals; Richard Henderson founds company to develop a new colony called Transylvania; Boone and 30 axmen blaze the Wilderness Road; Boonesborough is founded; Boone moves his family to Kentucky; Revolutionary War begins. |
| **1779** | More than 20,000 settlers travel over the Wilderness Road to Kentucky. |
| **1783** | The Revolution ends, giving Americans the opportunity to move west in large numbers. |
| **1792** | Kentucky becomes the 15th state. |
| **1795** | Governor Isaac Shelby orders the widening of the Wilderness Road. |
| **1940** | Cumberland Gap National Historical Park is created. |

# IMPORTANT PEOPLE

### DANIEL BOONE (1734–1820)
*Led the crew that blazed the Wilderness Road and settled in Kentucky with his family*

### RICHARD HENDERSON (1735–1785)
*Hired Daniel Boone to blaze the Wilderness Road*

### ISAAC SHELBY (1750–1826)
*First governor of the state of Kentucky; decided to widen the Wilderness Road to increase trade and travel*

### DR. THOMAS WALKER (1715–1794)
*Journeyed through and named Cave Gap (later Cumberland Gap); his reports led to maps of the region that helped settlers reach Kentucky*

# WANT TO KNOW MORE?

## At the Library

Calvert, Patricia. *Daniel Boone: Beyond the Mountains.* New York:
    Benchmark Books, 2002.

Green, Carl R. *Blazing the Wilderness Road with Daniel Boone in American
    History.* Berkeley Heights, N.J.: Enslow Publishers, 2000.

Stefoff, Rebecca. *First Frontier.* Tarrytown, N.Y.: Benchmark Books, 2001.

## On the Web

For more information on *The Wilderness Road*, use FactHound
to track down Web sites related to this book.

1. Go to *www.facthound.com*

2. Type in a search word related to this book
    or this book ID: 0756516374

3. Click on the *Fetch It* button.

FactHound will find Web sites related to this book.

## On the Road

**Cumberland Gap National
Historical Park**
U.S. Highway 25E South
P.O. Box 1848
Middlesboro, KY 40965
606/248-2817
Exhibits on the history of the area
and a restored section of the old
Wilderness Road

**Fort Boonesborough State Park**
4375 Boonesborough Road
Richmond, KY 40475
859/527-3131
A reconstructed fort, which includes
cabins, blockhouses, and furnishings;
pioneer artists demonstrate 18th-
century crafts

## Look for more We the People books about this era:

*The Alamo*
ISBN 0-7565-0097-4

*The Arapaho and Their History*
ISBN 0-7565-0831-2

*The Battle of the Little Bighorn*
ISBN 0-7565-0150-4

*The Buffalo Soldiers*
ISBN 0-7565-0833-9

*The California Gold Rush*
ISBN 0-7565-0041-9

*California Ranchos*
ISBN 0-7565-1633-1

*The Cherokee and Their History*
ISBN 0-7565-1273-5

*The Chumash and Their History*
ISBN 0-7565-0835-5

*The Creek and Their History*
ISBN 0-7565-0836-3

*The Erie Canal*
ISBN 0-7565-0679-4

*Great Women of Pioneer America*
ISBN 0-7565-1269-7

*Great Women of the Old West*
ISBN 0-7565-0099-0

*The Iroquois and Their History*
ISBN 0-7565-1272-7

*The Klondike Gold Rush*
ISBN 0-7565-1630-7

*The Lewis and Clark Expedition*
ISBN 0-7565-0044-3

*The Library of Congress*
ISBN 0-7565-1631-5

*The Louisiana Purchase*
ISBN 0-7565-0210-1

*The Mexican War*
ISBN 0-7565-0841-X

*The Ojibwe and Their History*
ISBN 0-7565-0843-6

*The Oregon Trail*
ISBN 0-7565-0045-1

*The Pony Express*
ISBN 0-7565-0301-9

*The Powhatan and Their History*
ISBN 0-7565-0844-4

*The Pueblo and Their History*
ISBN 0-7565-1274-3

*The Santa Fe Trail*
ISBN 0-7565-0047-8

*The Sioux and Their History*
ISBN 0-7565-1275-1

*The Trail of Tears*
ISBN 0-7565-0101-6

*The Transcontinental Railroad*
ISBN 0-7565-0153-9

*The Wampanoag and Their History*
ISBN 0-7565-0847-9

*The War of 1812*
ISBN 0-7565-0848-7

A complete list of We the People titles is available on our Web site:
www.compasspointbooks.com

# INDEX

## About the Author

Sarah De Capua is the author of many books, including nonfiction, biographies, geography, and historical titles. While researching this book, she enjoyed hiking old portions of the Wilderness Road, as well as discovering facts about the lives and journeys of the settlers who moved to Kentucky.